anythink

D0471399

EARLY PHYSICS FUN
SLIDES

by Jenny Fretland VanVoorst

pogo

Ideas for Parents and Teachers

Pogo Books let children practice reading informational text while introducing them to nonfiction features such as headings, labels, sidebars, maps, and diagrams, as well as a table of contents, glossary, and index.

Carefully leveled text with a strong photo match offers early fluent readers the support they need to succeed.

Before Reading

- "Walk" through the book and point out the various nonfiction features. Ask the student what purpose each feature serves.
- Look at the glossary together. Read and discuss the words.

Read the Book

- Have the child read the book independently.
- Invite him or her to list questions that arise from reading.

After Reading

- Discuss the child's questions. Talk about how he or she might find answers to those questions.
- Prompt the child to think more. Ask: Have you ever been on a blanket slide? How about a water slide? How did they compare with a regular playground slide? Were they faster? More fun?

Pogo Books are published by Jump!
5357 Penn Avenue South
Minneapolis, MN 55419
www.jumplibrary.com

Library of Congress Cataloging-in-Publication Data

Names: Fretland VanVoorst, Jenny, 1972- author.
Title: Slides / by Jenny Fretland VanVoorst.
Description: Minneapolis, MN : Jump!, Inc. [2016] |
Series: Early physics fun | Audience: Ages 7-10. |
Includes bibliographical references and index.
Identifiers: LCCN 2015045029| ISBN 9781620313183
(hardcover: alk. paper) | ISBN 9781624963704 (ebook)
Subjects: LCSH: Friction–Juvenile literature. |
Force and energy–Juvenile literature. | Physics–Study and teaching–Juvenile literature.
Classification: LCC QC197.F74 2016 | DDC 531–dc23
LC record available at http://lccn.loc.gov/2015045029

Series Editor: Jenny Fretland VanVoorst
Series Designer: Anna Peterson
Photo Researcher: Anna Peterson

Photo Credits: All photos by Shutterstock except:
Dreamstime, 10-11; Getty, 5, 16-17; iStock, cover, 1, 3, 8-9, 14-15, 19, 23.

Printed in the United States of America at Corporate Graphics in North Mankato, Minnesota.

TABLE OF CONTENTS

CHAPTER 1
Energy 4

CHAPTER 2
Gravity vs. Friction 12

CHAPTER 3
Newton's First Law 18

ACTIVITIES & TOOLS
Try This! 22
Glossary 23
Index 24
To Learn More 24

ENERGY

Slides are fun to play on. Most any playground has one. They can also teach you a lot about **physics**.

Physics is the science of matter and how it moves. There are physics **laws** by which all things work. Even slides!

A slide is like a long ramp. It is a simple machine. What's that? A simple machine uses physics **principles** to make work easier. And in the case of slides, they can also be used for fun!

DID YOU KNOW?

What are some other simple machines? Wheels and axles. **Pulleys**. **Levers**.

ramp

peak potential
energy

Sliding uses two kinds of energy. At the top of a slide, you have **potential energy**. Potential energy is based on location. It exists in anything that can move.

As you slide, potential energy becomes **kinetic energy**. That's the fun energy. Anything in motion has kinetic energy.

potential
energy

high
kinetic
energy

CHAPTER 2

GRAVITY VS. FRICTION

Gravity is a constant **force**. It pulls anything with mass back toward Earth. The more mass something has, the more gravity affects it.

Gravity plays an important role in determining kinetic energy. Why?

When you sit at the top of a slide, it's gravity that pulls you downward. Without gravity, a slide would be no fun.

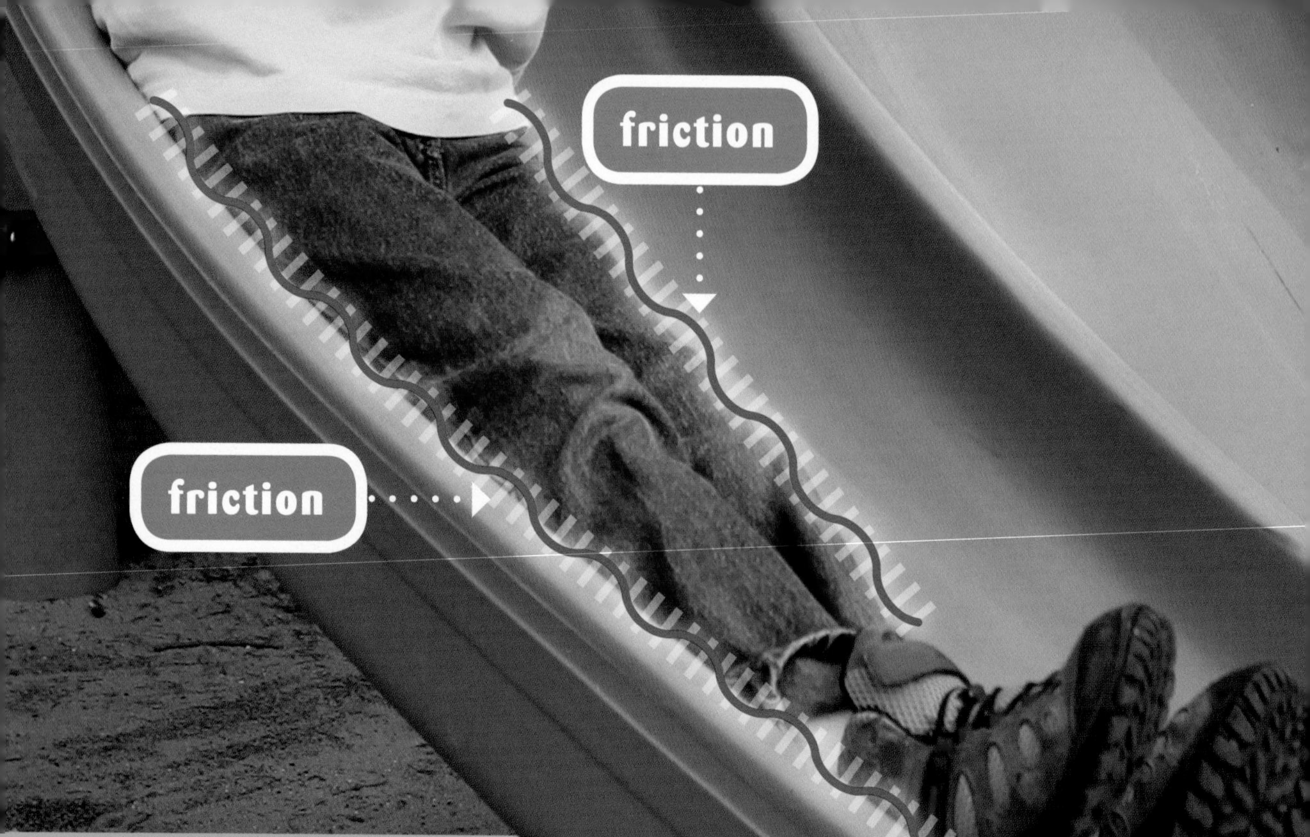

friction

friction

As you slide, **friction** keeps kinetic energy in check. Friction occurs whenever two objects rub against each other. When you slide, your clothing rubs against the slide. The materials resist each other. This keeps gravity from pulling you down the slide too quickly.

TAKE A LOOK!

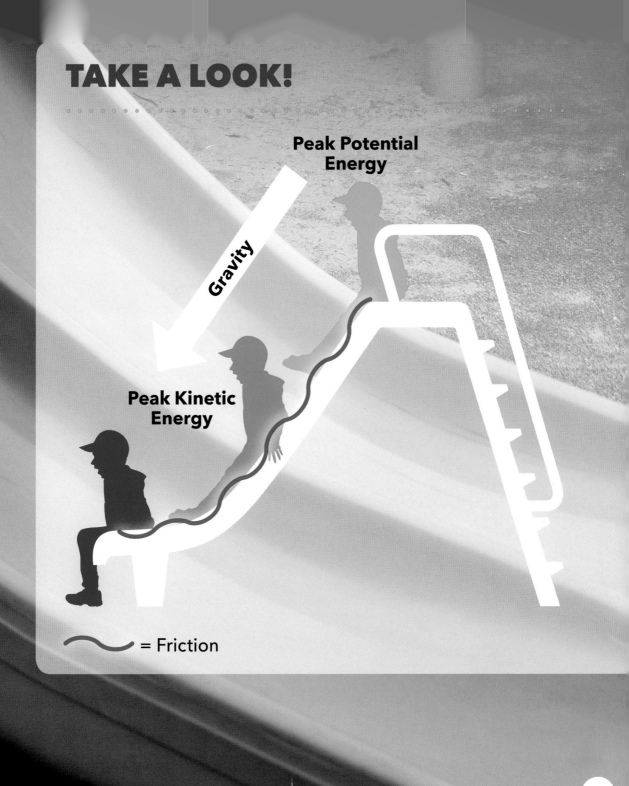

Peak Potential Energy

Gravity

Peak Kinetic Energy

〰 = Friction

CHAPTER 3

NEWTON'S FIRST LAW

Newton's First Law of Motion is one of the most famous laws of physics. It states that an object moves or rests until acted upon by an outside force. So what does this have to do with slides?

Imagine you are sitting at the top of the slide. You are at rest. You will stay at rest until you are pushed. Maybe a friend shoves you. Maybe you push yourself.

Once you are moving, you do so until something stops you. It's usually the ground at the bottom of the slide.

So go outside and play with physics. Now you know a slide is not such a simple machine after all.

ACTIVITIES & TOOLS

FRICTION TEST

Let's see how friction affects kinetic energy. You will need access to a playground slide and a few additional items:

- rubber bath mat
- soft fleece blanket

1 First slide down the slide with nothing between your clothes and the surface of the slide.

2 Now slide while sitting on something that will reduce friction, such as a soft blanket.

3 Now slide down on something that will increase friction, such as a rubber bath mat.

4 Compare the experiences. Which was faster? Which was more fun? How do you think friction affects kinetic energy?

GLOSSARY

force: An influence (as a push or pull) that tends to produce a change in the speed or direction of motion of something.

friction: The force that resists motion between bodies in contact.

gravity: The attraction of the earth for bodies at or near its surface.

kinetic energy: Energy associated with motion.

laws: Scientific rules.

lever: A stiff bar for applying a force at one point of its length by applying effort at a second point.

mass: The quantity of matter in a body; it differs from weight in that weight is a measurement of the force of gravity on a mass.

Newton's First Law of Motion: The physics law that states that unless acted upon by an outside force, an object in motion tends to stay in motion at the same speed and direction.

physics: The area of science that has to do with matter and how it moves through space and time.

potential energy: Energy associated with location.

principle: A law or fact of nature which makes possible the working of a machine or device.

pulley: A small wheel used with a rope or chain to change the direction of a pulling force.

INDEX

force 12, 18

friction 16, 17

gravity 12, 13, 14, 16, 17

kinetic energy 10, 13, 16, 17

laws 5, 18

levers 6

location 9

mass 10, 12, 14

matter 5, 14

motion 10, 18

Newton's First Law of Motion 18

physics 4, 5, 6, 18, 20

playground 4

potential energy 9, 10, 17

pulleys 6

ramp 6

rest 18, 19

simple machine 6, 20

weight 10, 14

wheels and axles 6

TO LEARN MORE

Learning more is as easy as 1, 2, 3.

1) Go to www.factsurfer.com

2) Enter "slides" into the search box.

3) Click the "Surf" button to see a list of websites.

With factsurfer, finding more information is just a click away.